The Seven Lamps of Sanctification

Catechesis on the Virtues of the Christian Life

The Seven Lamps of Sanctification

Catechesis on the Virtues of the Christian Life

Pope Blessed John Paul I
and
Pope Saint John Paul II

Edited by
Geoffrey W.M.P. Lopes da Silva

Domina Nostra Publishing
Providence, Rhode Island, USA

Published in 2023 by
Domina Nostra Publishing
555 N. Main Street, #1329
Providence, RI. 02904-5722 USA
Email: info@DominaNostraPublishing.com
Website: www.DominaNostraPublishing.com

Copyright © 2023 Dicastery for Communication / Libreria Editrice Vaticana
Copyright © 2023 Domina Nostra Publishing

Printed and bound in the United States of America.
All rights reserved.

The Latin scriptural texts are taken from the *Nova Vulgata, Bibliorum Sacrorum Editio*, editio typica altera 1986.

The English scriptural texts are taken from the Second Catholic Edition of the *Revised Standard Version of the Bible* (2006), copyright 1965, 1966, by the Division of Christian Education of the National Council of the Churches of Christ in the United States of America. Used by permission. All rights reserved.

Although the editor and publisher have made every effort to ensure the accuracy and completeness of information contained in this book, we assume no responsibility for errors, inaccuracies, omissions, or any inconsistency herein. Any slights of people, places, or organisations are unintentional. Attempt has been made to give proper credit to all sources used in the text, illustrations, and graphics. Any miscredit or lack of credit is unintended and will be corrected in a future edition.

First printing, 2023

ISBN 978-0-9741900-9-9

« *Sit finis vitæ cum virtute degendæ,
ut quis Numini divino assimiletur* »

"May the end of life be spent with virtue,
so that one may be assimilated to the divine spirit".[1]

Saint Gregory of Nazianzus
(AD 329-390)
De beatitudinibus, oratio 1:
Patrologia Graeca 44, 1200D

---

[1] The *Catechism of the Catholic Church, Second Edition* (1997) translates this as "The goal of a virtuous life is to become like God" (n. 1803).

Pope John Paul I,
263rd Bishop of Rome
and
Karol Józef Cardinal Wojtyła,
76th Archbishop of Kraków

3 September 1978

CONTENTS

Preface   9

Introduction   11

Part I
Catechesis on the Theological Virtues
by Pope Blessed John Paul I

1. Faith   16
2. Hope   22
3. Charity   27

Part II
Catechesis on the Cardinal Virtues
by Pope Saint John Paul II

4. Prudence   34
5. Justice   38
6. Fortitude   42
7. Temperance   46

Appendices

I. Acts of the Theological Virtues   52
   Actus virtutum theologalium

II. Prayer Saint Thomas Aquinas to Acquire the Virtues   53

Indices

Index of Scriptural Citations   56
Index of Names   57

Preface

On Wednesday, 13 September 1978, Blessed John Paul I began a series of catechesis on what Pope Saint John XXIII called "*le sette lampade della santificazione*", Italian for "the seven lamps of sanctification". These "seven lamps" consist of the three theological virtues of faith, hope, and charity, and the four cardinal virtues of prudence, justice, fortitude, and temperance. These seven virtues are the foundation and energizing force of a Christian's moral activity and serve as the pillars of a virtuous life.

Holy Mother Church teaches that the three theological virtues originate from God Himself and are infused with sanctifying grace, which empowers individuals to enter into a relationship with the Most Blessed Trinity. The human virtues, on the other hand, are habitual and stable perfections of the intellect and will that regulate our actions, order our passions, and guide our behaviour according to faith and reason. These virtues are acquired and strengthened through the repetition of morally good acts and purified and elevated by divine grace. The principal human virtues are known as the cardinal virtues, and form the foundation for all other virtues.

Blessed John Paul I's reign lasted only 33 days. Upon his election to the Chair of Peter, Saint John Paul the Great continued his predecessor's catechesis, bringing it to its natural conclusion on Wednesday, 22 November 1978.

It is my hope that this book will help Christians to live a life of virtue, thereby becoming more like God.

Geoffrey W.M.P. Lopes da Silva
Publisher and Executive Editor

28 May 2023
Dominica Pentecostes

Introduction

The Seven Lamps of Sanctification: Catechesis on the Virtues of the Christian Life collects the addresses given by Blessed Pope John Paul I at the weekly general audiences from 13 September 1978 until his death on 28 September 1978. Saint Pope John Paul II resumed the series on 25 October 1978 and brought it to its natural conclusion on 22 November 1978.

The paragraphs of Blessed John Paul I's original Italian texts were not numbered and Saint John Paul II's catecheses of 8 and 22 November were the only ones to have numbered paragraphs. The editor has numbered them according to the number of paragraphs corresponding to the original for ease of reference. The English texts have been adapted to the original Italian formatting whenever applicable.

Each catechesis is subtitled with a quotation from the 1997 edition of the *Catechismus Catholicæ Ecclesiæ (Catechism of the Catholic Church)*, which provides a clear and concise definition of the virtue being discussed. These quotations are in italics and do not form part of the official catechetical address.

All footnotes in this book are the editor's own.

His Late Holiness Pope
BLESSED JOHN PAUL I
(*Beatus Ioannes Paulus primus*),
Sovereign Pontiff, Bishop of Rome, Vicar of Jesus Christ,
Successor of the Prince of the Apostles,
Supreme Pontiff of the Universal Church,
Patriarch of the West, Primate of Italy,
Archbishop and Metropolitan of the Roman Province,
Sovereign of the State of Vatican City,
Servant of the Servants of God.

~~~~~~~~~~~~~~~~~~~~~~~

ALBINO LUCIANI was born on 17 October 1912 in Forno di Canale (Canale d'Agordo), Italy, and ordained to the priesthood on 7 July 1935. He was appointed the 37th Bishop of Vittorio Veneto on 15 December 1958 by Pope St John XXIII (1881-1963) and was ordained (consecrated) bishop on 27 December 1958. He was a Father of the Second Vatican Ecumenical Council (1962-1965) and was appointed the 77th Patriarch of Venice in Italy on 15 December 1969 by Pope St Paul VI (1897-1978).

Elevated to the Sacred College of Cardinals and appointed Cardinal-Priest of San Marco on 5 March 1973, he was styled as the Most Eminent and Most Reverend Lord, Lord Albino Cardinal of the Holy Roman Church Luciani.

"Papa Luciani" was elected the 263rd Bishop of Rome and the 262nd Successor of Saint Peter on 26 August 1978. He solemnly initiated the Petrine Ministry in Saint Peter's Square on 3 September 1978.

On 28 September 1978, Pope Blessed John Paul I died in the Apostolic Palace and was buried on 4 October 1978 in the Basilica of Saint Peter's at the Vatican.

His cause of Beatification and Canonisation was opened on 26 August 2002 and he was posthumously styled Servant of God. He was recognized to have lived a heroic and virtuous life and was proclaimed Venerable on 8 November 2017. He was beatified on 4 September 2022 by Pope Francis.

His feast day is celebrated on 26 August.

His Late Holiness Pope
SAINT JOHN PAUL II
(Sanctus Ioannes Paulus secundus),
Sovereign Pontiff, Bishop of Rome, Vicar of Jesus Christ,
Successor of the Prince of the Apostles,
Supreme Pontiff of the Universal Church,
Patriarch of the West, Primate of Italy,
Archbishop and Metropolitan of the Roman Province,
Sovereign of the State of Vatican City,
Servant of the Servants of God.

~~~~~~~~~~~~~~~~~~~~~~~~

KAROL JÓZEF WOTJTYŁA was born on 18 May 1920 in Wadowice, Poland, and ordained to the priesthood on 1 November 1946. He was appointed Auxiliary Bishop of Kraków on 5 July 1958 by Pope Ven. Pius XII (1876-1958) and was ordained (consecrated) bishop (Titular Bishop of Ombi) on 28 September 1958. He was appointed the 76th Archbishop of Kraków on 13 January 1964 by Pope St Paul VI (1897-1978). He was also a Father of the Second Vatican Ecumenical Council (1962-1965).

Elevated to the Sacred College of Cardinals and appointed Cardinal-Priest of San Cesareo in Palatio on 26 June 1967, he was styled as the Most Eminent and Most Reverend Lord, Lord Karol Józef Cardinal of the Holy Roman Church Wotjtyła.

"Papa Wotjtyła" was elected the 264th Bishop of Rome and the 263rd Successor of Saint Peter on 16 October 1978. He solemnly initiated the Petrine Ministry in Saint Peter's Square on 22 October 1978.

On 2 April 2005, the Saturday in the Octave of Easter and the Vigil of the Sunday of Divine Mercy, Pope Saint John Paul II died in the Apostolic Palace and was buried on 8 April 2005, in the Basilica of Saint Peter's at the Vatican.

His cause of Beatification and Canonisation was opened on 28 June 2005 and he was posthumously styled Servant of God. He was recognized to have lived a heroic and virtuous life and was proclaimed Venerable on 19 December 2009. He was beatified on 1 May 2011 by Pope Benedict XVI and canonized on 27 April 2014 by Pope Francis.

His feast day is celebrated on 22 October.

Part I
The Theological Virtues

Pope Blessed John Paul I

1
The Virtue of Faith

By faith, we believe in God and believe all that He has revealed to us and that Holy Church proposes for our belief.[1]

1. My first greeting goes to my brother bishops, of whom I see many here.

   Pope John,[2] in a note of his, which was also published, said: "This time I gave the retreat on the Seven Lamps of Sanctification".[3] Seven virtues, he meant, that is, faith, hope, charity, prudence, justice, fortitude, temperance. Who knows if the Holy Spirit will help the poor Pope today to illustrate at least one of these lamps, the first one, faith.

   Here in Rome there was a poet, Trilussa,[4] who also tried to speak of faith. In a certain poem of his, he said:

   > That little old blind woman, whom I met
   > the evening I lost my way in the middle of the wood,
   > said to me: —If you don't know the way
   > I'll accompany you, for I know it
   > If you have the strength to follow me
   > from time to time I'll call to you,
   > right to the bottom there, where there is a cypress,
   > right to the top there, where there is a cross.
   > I answered: that may be... but I find it strange
   > that I can be guided by someone sightless...
   > The blind woman, then, took my hand
   > and sighed: Come on. — It was faith.[5]

   As a poem, it is delightful; as theology, defective.

---

[1] « *Fide credimus in Deum atque omnia credimus quæ Ipse nobis revelavit quæque Ecclesia nobis proponit credenda* » (*Catechismus Catholicæ Ecclesiæ*, editio typica 1997, n. 1842).

[2] Pope Saint John XXIII (*Sanctus Ioannes XXIII*) was born Angelo Giuseppe Roncalli in 1881 and elected the 261st Bishop of Rome in 1958. He summoned the Second Vatican Council in 1962 and died in 1963. He was beatified by Pope St John Paul the Great in 2000 and canonized by Pope Francis in 2014. His feast day is 11 October, the anniversary of the opening of the Council.

[3] Original Italian: « *Stavolta ho fatto il ritiro sulle sette lampade della santificazione* ».

[4] Carlo Alberto Salustri 1873-1950) was an Italian poet, better known by his pen name of Trilussa, which is an anagram of his surname. He is best known for the poems, some of them sonnets, written in the Roman dialect.

[5] *La Fede* [Faith].

It is defective because when it is a question of faith, the great stage manager is God. Because Jesus said: "No one comes to me unless my Father draws him".[1] Saint Paul did not have faith, in fact he was persecuting the faithful. God waits for him on the way to Damascus: "Paul", he says to him, "don't take it into your head to rear up, to kick, like a restive horse. I am that Jesus whom you are persecuting. I need you. You must change!" Paul surrendered; he changed, leading a completely different life. Some years afterwards, he will write to the Philippians: "that time, on the way to Damascus, God seized me; since then I have done nothing but run after him, to see if I, too, am able to seize him, imitating him, loving him more and more".[2]

That is what faith is: to surrender to God, but transforming one's life. A thing that is not always easy! Augustine[3] has told of the journey of his faith; especially in the last few weeks it was terrible; reading, one feels his soul almost shudder and writhe in interior conflicts. On the one hand, God calls him and insists; on the other hand, his old habits, "old friends", he writes...; "and they pulled me gently by my mantle of flesh and they said to me: 'Augustine, what! You are abandoning us? Look out, you won't be able to do this anymore, you won't be able ever again to do that other.'" A hard thing! "I felt", he says, "like one who is in bed, in the morning. He is told: 'Out, Augustine, get up! Finally the Lord gave me a sharp tug, and I came out. You see, one mustn't say: 'Yes, but; yes, but later'. One must say: 'Yes, Lord! At once!' This is faith. To respond to the Lord generously. But who says this 'yes'? He who is humble and trusts God completely!"

2. My mother used to tell me when I was a boy: "When you were little, you were very ill. I had to take you from one doctor to another and watch over you whole nights; do you believe me?" How could I have said: "I don't believe you, Mamma? Of course I believe, I believe what you tell me, but I believe especially in you".

And so it is in faith. It is not just a question of believing in the things that God revealed, but in him who deserves our faith, who has loved us so much and done so much for our sake.

---

[1] "*Nemo potest venire ad me, nisi Pater, qui misit me, traxerit eum*" (*Ioannem* 6, 44); "No one can come to me unless the Father who sent me draws him" (*Revised Standard Version of the Bible, Second Catholic Edition = RSV-2CE*).
[2] The Conversion of Saint Paul of Tarsus, cf. *Acts* 9:3-6, *1 Corinthians* 15:3-8, and *Galatians* 1:11-16.
[3] Saint Augustine of Hippo (354-439) was Bishop of Hippo in North Africa and is a Doctor of the Church. His feast day is 28 August.

It is also difficult to accept some truths, because the truths of faith are of two kinds; some pleasant, others unpalatable to our spirit. For example, it is pleasant to hear that God has so much tenderness for us, even more tenderness than a mother has for her children, as Isaiah says. How pleasant and congenial it is! There was a great French bishop, Dupanloup,[1] who used to say to the rectors of seminaries: "with the future priests, be fathers, be mothers". It is agreeable. Other truths, on the contrary, are hard to accept. God must punish, if I resist. He runs after me, he begs me to repent and I say: "No!" I almost force him to punish me. This is not agreeable. But it is a truth of faith. And there is a last difficulty, the Church. Saint Paul asked: "Who are you, Lord?" — "I am Jesus, whom you are persecuting".[2]

3. A light, a flash, crossed his mind. I do not persecute Jesus, I don't even know him: I persecute the Christians. It is clear that Jesus and the Christians, Jesus and the Church are the same thing: indissoluble, inseparable.

4. Read Saint Paul: "*Corpus Christi quod est Ecclesia*".[3] Christ and the Church are only one thing. Christ is the Head, we, the Church, are his limbs. It is not possible to have faith and to say, "I believe in Jesus, I accept Jesus but I do not accept the Church". We must accept the Church, as she is. And what is this Church like? Pope John called her "*Mater et Magistra*".[4] Teacher also. Saint Paul said: "Let everyone accept us as Christ's aids and stewards and dispensers of his mysteries".[5]

5. When the poor Pope, when the bishops, the priests, propose the doctrine, they are merely helping Christ. It is not our doctrine, it is Christ's; we

---

[1] Félix Antoine Philibert Dupanloup (1802-1878), 25th Bishop of Orléans in France and one of the fathers of the First Vatican Council (1869-1870).

[2] "*Quis es, Domine?*" — "*Ego sum Iesus, quem tu persequeris!*" (*Actus Apostolorum* 9, 5).

[3] Cf. *Romans* 12:3-5, *1 Corinthians* 12:12, *Ephesians* 1:22-23, 5:29-30. "*Corpus Christi, quod est Ecclesia* [*The Body of Christ, which is the Church*]" is the title of a 1946 book written in Latin by Sebastiaan P.C. Tromp, SJ (1889-1975), a Dutch Jesuit priest, theologian, and Latinist. He is best known for assisting Venerable Pius XII with his theological encyclicals and Pope St John XXIII in the preparation for the Second Vatican Council. He was an assistant to Alfredo Cardinal Ottaviani during the Council and professor of Catholic theology at the Pontifical Gregorian University from 1929 until 1967.

[4] *Mater et Magistra* [Mother and Teacher] is the Latin title for the encyclical letter on Christianity and Social Progress of Pope St John XXIII, promulgated in 1961; *Acta Apostolicae Sedis* (= *AAS*) 53 [1961], pp. 401-464.

[5] "*Sic nos existimet homo ut mi nistros Christi et dispensatores mysteriorum Dei*" (*1 Corinthios* 4, 1); "This is how one should regard us, as servants of Christ and stewards of the mysteries of God" (*RSV-2CE*).

must just guard it and present it. I was present when Pope John opened the Council on 11 October 1962. At a certain point he said: "We hope that with the Council the Church will take a leap forward".[1] We all hoped so; but a leap forward, on what way? He told us at once: on certain and immutable truths. It never even occurred to Pope John that the truths could go forward, and then, gradually, change. Those are the truths: we must walk along the way of these truths, understanding them more and more, bringing ourselves up-to-date, proposing them in a form suited to the new times. Pope Paul too had the same thought. The first thing I did, as soon as I was made Pope, was to enter the private Chapel of the Pontifical Household. Right at the back Pope Paul had two mosaics made: Saint Peter and Saint Paul: Saint Peter dying, Saint Paul dying. But under Saint Peter are the words of Jesus: "I will pray for you, Peter, that your faith may never fail".[2] Under Saint Paul, on whom the sword falls: "I have finished the race, I have kept the faith".[3] You know that in his last address on 29 June, Paul VI[4] said: "After fifteen years of pontificate, I can thank the Lord that I have defended the faith, that I have kept the faith".[5]

6. The Church is also a mother. If she continues Christ, and Christ is good, the Church too must be good; good to everyone. But if by chance there should sometimes be bad people in the Church? We have our mother. If mother is sick, if my mother by chance should become lame, I love her even more. It is the same, in the Church. If there are, and there are, defects and shortcomings, our affection for the Church must never fail. Yesterday, and I conclude, I was sent the issue of "*Città Nuova*".[6] I saw that they have reported, recording it, a very short address of mine, with

---

[1] "*Huius ergo Concilii lumine illustrata, Ecclesia spiritualibus divitiis, ut confidimus, augebitur atque, novarum virium robur ex illo hauriens, intrepide futura prospiciet tempora*" (SANCTUS IOANNES XXIII, *Allocutio in sollemni SS. Concili inauguratione* [*Address on the occasion of the solemn opening of the Most Holy Council*] (11 octobris 1962), n. 3.4: *AAS* 54 (1962), n. 14, p. 788).

[2] "*Ego autem rogavi pro te, ut non deficiat fides tua*" (*Lucam* 22, 32); "but I have prayed for you that your faith may not fail" (*RSV-2CE*).

[3] "*Cursum consummavi, fidem servavi*" (*2 Timotheum* 4, 7).

[4] Pope Saint Paul VI (*Sanctus Paulus VI*) was born Giovanni Battista Enrico Antonio Maria Montini in 1897 and elected the 262nd Bishop of Rome in 1963. He continued the Second Vatican Council (1962-1965) and died in 1978. He was beatified in 2014 and canonized in 2018.

[5] SAINT PAUL VI, *Homily*, 29 June 1978 (Solemnity of Saints Peter and Paul): *Acta Apostolicae Sedis* 70 [1978], 394-399.

[6] *Città Nuova* [Italian: *New City*] is the monthly magazine of the Focolare Movement or Work of Mary (*Movimento dei Focolari o Opera di Maria*), founded in 1943 by Chiara Lubich (1920-2008).

an episode. A certain British preacher MacNabb,[1] speaking in Hyde Park, had spoken of the Church. When he finished, someone asked to speak and said: "Yours are fine words. But I know some Catholic priests who did not stay with the poor and became rich. I know also Catholic husbands who have betrayed their wives. I do not like this Church made of sinners". The Father said: "There's something in what you say. But may I make an objection?" — "Let's hear it". — He says: "Excuse me, but am I mistaken or is the collar of your shirt a little greasy?" — He says: "Yes, it is, I admit". — "But is it greasy because you haven't used soap, or because you used soap, but it was no use?" "No", he says, I haven't used soap".

You see. The Catholic Church too has extraordinary soap: the gospel, the sacraments, prayer. The gospel read and lived; the sacraments celebrated in the right way; prayer well used, would be a marvellous soap, capable of making us all saints. We are not all saints, because we have not used this soap enough. Let us try to meet the hopes of the Popes who held and applied the Council, Pope John, Pope Paul. Let us try to improve the Church, by becoming better ourselves. Each of us and the whole Church could recite the prayer I am accustomed to recite: "Lord, take me as I am, with my defects, with my shortcomings, but make me become as You want me to be".

7. I must say a word also to our dear sick, whom I see there. You know, Jesus said: "I hide behind them; what is done for them is done for me".[2] So we venerate the Lord himself in their persons and we hope that the Lord will be close to them and help and sustain them.

8. On our right, on the other hand, there are the newlyweds. They have received a great sacrament. Let us wish that this sacrament which they have received will really bring not only goods of this world, but more spiritual graces. Last century there was in France a great professor, Frederick Ozanam.[3] He taught at the Sorbonne, and was so eloquent, so capable!

---

[1] Rev. Vincent McNabb (1868-1943), Irish, member of the Order of Preachers (Dominicans), scholar, and apologist. He has been called a Master of Sacred Theology and "the Saint of Hyde Park".
[2] Cf. *Matthew* 25:31-46.
[3] Blessed Antoine-Frédéric Ozanam (1813-1853) was a French scholar who co-founded the Society of Saint Vincent de Paul (Société de Saint-Vincent-de-Paul) in 1833. He was beatified by Pope St John Paul II in the Cathedral of Notre Dame de Paris in 1997. His feast day is 9 September.

His friend was Lacordaire,[1] who said: "He is so gifted, he is so good, he will become a priest, he will become a great bishop, this fellow!" No! He met a nice girl and they got married, Lacordaire was disappointed and said: "Poor Ozanam! He too has fallen into the trap!" But two years later, Lacordaire came to Rome, and was received by Pius IX.[2] "Come, come, Father", he says. "I have always heard that Jesus established seven sacraments. Now you come along and change everything. You tell me that he established six sacraments, and a trap! No, Father, marriage is not a trap, it is a great sacrament!" So let us express again our best wishes for these dear newlyweds: may the Lord bless them!

Blessed John Paul I
13 September 1978

---

[1] Jean-Baptiste Henri-Dominique Lacordaire (1802–1861) was "the greatest pulpit orator of the nineteenth century" (*The Catholic Encyclopedia*, 1910). In 1837, he undertook to re-establish the Order of Preachers (Dominicans) in post-Revolutionary France.

[2] Pope Blessed Pius IX (1792-1878), born Giovanni Maria Mastai-Ferretti, was elected the 255th Bishop of Rome on 16 June 1846. He reigned for nearly 32 years, making his papacy the longest in the history of the Church. He defined *ex cathedra* the dogma of the Immaculate Conception of the Blessed Virgin Mary in 1854 and convened the First Vatican Council in 1869 which decreed the dogma of Papal Infallibility. In the 1950s and again in 2000, the body of Blessed Pius IX was found to be incorrupt. He was beatified by Pope St John Paul II in 2000. His feast day is 7 February.

2
The Virtue of Hope

*By hope we desire, and with steadfast trust await from God,
eternal life and the graces to merit it.*[1]

1. The second of the seven "Lamps of Sanctification" for Pope John was Hope. Today I will speak to you of this virtue, which is obligatory for every Christian. In his *Paradiso*, Dante[2] imagined himself taking an examination in Christianity (Dante Alighieri, *La Divina Commedia*, "*Paradiso*", XXIV, XXV, XXVI). A magnificent commission was operating. "Do you have faith?" Saint Peter asks him first. "Do you have hope?" Saint James continues. "Do you have charity?" Saint John ends. "Yes", Dante answers, "I have faith, I have hope, I have charity". He proves it and passes with full marks. I said that hope is obligatory: that does not mean that hope is ugly or hard. On the contrary, anyone who lives it travels in an atmosphere of trust and abandonment, saying with the psalmist:

   "Lord, you are my rock, my shield, my fortress, my refuge, my lamp, my shepherd, my salvation. Even if an army were to encamp against me, my heart will not fear; and if the battle rises against me, even then I am confident".[3]

2. You will say: is not this psalmist exaggeratedly enthusiastic? Is it possible that things always went right for him? No, they did not always go right. He, too, knows, and says so, that the bad are often fortunate and the good oppressed. He even complained to the Lord about it sometimes; he went so far as to say: "Why are you sleeping, Lord? Why are you silent? Wake up, listen to me, Lord".[4] But his hope remained: firm, unshakeable. To him and to all those who hope can be applied what Saint Paul said of Abraham: "In hope he believed against hope" (*Rom* 4:18).[5] You will say further: how can this happen? It happens

---

[1] « *Spe cupimus et a Deo exspectamus, cum firma fiducia, vitam æternam et gratias ad illam merendam* » (*Catechismus Catholicæ Ecclesiæ*, editio typica 1997, n. 1843).

[2] Durante degli Alighieri (ca. 1265-1321), was a major Italian poet of the Middle Ages. His Divine Comedy, originally called *Commedia* and later called *Divina* by Boccaccio, is widely considered the greatest literary work composed in the Italian language and a masterpiece of world literature. In Italy he is known as *il Sommo Poeta* ("the Supreme Poet") or just *il Poeta* and "Father of the Italian language".

[3] Cf. *Psalm* 17 (18):3 and *Psalm* 26 (27):3.

[4] Cf. *Psalm* 34 (35):22-23.

[5] "*Qui contra spem in spe credidit*" (*Romanos* 4, 18).

because one is attached to three truths: God is almighty, God loves me immensely, God is faithful to promises. And it is he, the God of mercy, who kindles trust in me; so that I do not feel lonely, or useless, or abandoned, but involved in a destiny of salvation, which will lead to Paradise one day. I mentioned the Psalms. The same certain confidence vibrates in the books of the Saints. I would like you to read a homily delivered by Saint Augustine on Easter day about Alleluia. We will sing the true Alleluia: — he says approximately — in Paradise. That will be the Alleluia of full love: this one, now, is the Alleluia of starving love, that is, of hope.[1]

3. Someone will say: What if I am a poor sinner? I reply to him as I replied to an unknown lady, who had confessed to me many years ago. She was discouraged because, she said, she had a stormy life morally. "May I ask you", I said, "how old you are?" — "Thirty-five". — "Thirty-five! But you can live for another forty or fifty and do a great deal of good. So, repentant as you are, instead of thinking of the past, project yourself into the future and renew your life. With God's help". On that occasion I quoted Saint Francis de Sales,[2] who speaks of "our dear imperfections".[3] I explained: God detests failings because they are failings. On the other hand, however, in a certain sense he loves failings since they give to him an opportunity to show his mercy and to us an opportunity to remain humble and to understand and to sympathize with our neighbour's failings.

4. Not everyone shares this sympathy of mine for hope. Nietzsche,[4] for example, calls it the "virtue of the weak". According to him, it makes the Christian a useless, separated, resigned person, extraneous to the progress of the world. Others speak of "alienation", which, they say,

---

[1] Cf. Saint Augustine, Psalm 148: *The Liturgy of the Hours*, Saturday of the 5th Week of Easter, Office of Readings; *Corpus Christianorum, Series Latina* 40, 2165-2166.

[2] Saint Francis de Sales (1567-1622), 7th Bishop of Geneva (1602), Confessor, and Doctor of the Church. His most famous writings include *Introduction to the Devout Life* and *Treatise on the Love of God*. He founded the women's Order of the Visitation of Holy Mary (Visitandines) with Saint Jane Frances de Chantal in 1610. He was beatified in 1661 and canonised in 1665 by Pope Alexander VII and proclaimed patron saint of writers and journalists in 1923 by Pope Pius XI. His feast day is 24 January in the Ordinary Form of the Roman Rite and 29 January in the Extraordinary Form.

[3] "Dear imperfections, you make us accept our misery, practice both humility and contempt of ourselves, as well as patience and diligence" (Saint Francis de Sales, *Letter V*, To a Young Lady, On Perfection).

[4] Friedrich Wilhelm Nietzsche (1844-1900) was a German philosopher, poet, composer, cultural critic, and classical philologist. He wrote critical texts on religion, morality, contemporary culture, philosophy, and science, displaying a fondness for metaphor, irony, and aphorism.

turns the Christian away from the struggle for human advancement. But "the Christian message", the Council said, "far from deterring men from the task of building up the world... binds them, rather, to all this by a still more stringent obligation" (*Gaudium et Spes*, 34, cf. ibid. 39 and 57; cf. etiam M*essage to the World of the Council Fathers*, 20 October 1962).[1]

5. In the course of the centuries there have also appeared from time to time affirmations and tendencies of Christians that were too pessimistic with regard to man. But these affirmations were disapproved of by the Church and were forgotten, thanks to a host of joyful and hardworking saints, to Christian humanism, to the ascetic teachers, whom Saint-Beuve[2] called *"les doux"*,[3] and to a comprehensive theology. Saint Thomas Aquinas,[4] for example, puts among the virtues *iucunditas* or the capacity of changing things heard and seen into a cheerful smile—to the extent and in the way appropriate (cf. *S. Thomæ, Summa Theologiæ*, II-IIae, q. 168, a. 2). This kind of cheerfulness, I explained to my pupils, was shown by that Irish mason who fell from the scaffolding and broke his legs. He was taken to hospital and the doctor and Sister nurse rushed to him. "Poor thing", the latter said, "you hurt yourself falling". But I the patient said: "Mother, not exactly falling, but reaching the ground I hurt myself".

When Saint Thomas declared that joking and making people smile was a virtue, he was in agreement with the "glad-tidings"[5] preached by Christ, and with the *hilaritas*[6] recommended by Saint Augustine.

---

[1] "*Unde apparet christiano nuntio homines ab exstruendo mundo non averti, nec ad bonum sui similium negligendum impelli, sed potius officio hæc operandi arctius obstringi*" (CONCILIUM VATICANUM II, Const. past. de Ecclesia in mundo huius temporis, *Gaudium et spes*, 34: *AAS* 58 [1966], 1035).

[2] Charles Augustin Sainte-Beuve (1804-1869) was a literary critic of French literature.

[3] "*Les doux*" is French for "sweets".

[4] Saint Thomas Aquinas (1225-1274), member of the Order of Preachers (Dominicans), influential philosopher and theologian in the tradition of scholasticism, known as the "*Doctor Angelicus*", "*Doctor Communis*", and "*Doctor Universalis*". He was canonized in Avignon in 1323 by Pope John XXII and proclaimed a Doctor of the Church in 1567 by Pope Saint Pius V. His feast day is 28 January in the Ordinary Form of the Roman Rite and on 7 March in the Extraordinary Form.

[5] "Glad-tidings" or "good news" is the modern English translation for the Greek εὐαγγέλιον [*euangelion*] and Latin: *evangelium*. The English word gospel derives from the Old English godspel (cf. *Matthew* 11:5; *Luke* 4:1, 7:22, 9:6, 20:1).

[6] "Hilaritas, a bright and cheerful manner" (*The Catholic Encyclopedia* (1909), vol. 5); cf. SANCTUS AUGUSTINUS, *De catechizandis rudibus* [*Catechizing of the Uninstructed*]: *Patrologia Latina* (=*PL*), vol. 40, col. 309-348.

He overcame pessimism, clothed Christian life in joy and invited us to keep up our courage also with the healthy, pure joys, which we meet on our way.

When I was a boy, I read something about Andrew Carnegie the Scot,[1] who went to America with his parents and gradually became one of the richest men in the world. He was not a Catholic, but I was struck by the fact that he returned insistently to the simple, true joys of his life. "I was born in poverty", he said, "but I would not exchange the memories of my childhood with those of a millionaire's children. What do they know of family joys, of the sweet figure of a mother who combines the duties of nurse, washerwoman, cook, teacher, angel, and saint?" When still very young, he took a job in a Pittsburgh mill with 56 miserable *lire*[2] a month as wages. One evening, instead of giving him his wage at once, the cashier told him to wait. Carnegie was trembling: "Now they'll dismiss me".

On the contrary, after paying the others, the cashier said to him: "Andrew, I've watched your work carefully; I've come to the conclusion that it is worth more than that of the others. I'm raising your wage to 67 *lire*". Carnegie said many years afterwards, "all my millions put together never gave me the joy of that eleven lire rise".

Certainly, these joys, though good and encouraging, must not be absolutized. They are something, not everything; they serve as a means, they are not the supreme purpose; they do not last for ever, but only for a short time. "Christians", Saint Paul wrote, "deal with the world as though they had no dealings with it. For the form of this world is passing away" (cf. *1 Cor* 7:31).[3] Christ had already said: "Seek first of all the kingdom of God" (*Mt* 6:33).[4]

---

[1] Andrew Carnegie (1835-1919) was a Scottish-American industrialist who led the enormous expansion of the American steel industry in the late 19th century. He was also one of the highest profile philanthropists of his era, writing the 1889 article "Wealth". Also known as "The Gospel of Wealth", it describes the responsibility of philanthropy by the new upper class of the self-made rich.

[2] *Lire* is the plural for *Lira* (£), the name currency used in Italy, Vatican City, Malta, and San Marino until it was replaced by the euro in 2002.

[3] "*Et qui utuntur hoc mundo, tamquam non abutentes; praeterit enim figura huius mundi*" (*1 Corinthios* 7:31); "and those who deal with the world as though they had no dealings with it. For the form of this world is passing away" (*RSV-2CE*).

[4] "*Quærite autem primum regnum Dei et iustitiam eius*" (*Matthæum* 6, 33); "But seek first his kingdom and his righteousness" (*RSV-2CE*).

6. In conclusion, I would like to refer to a hope which is proclaimed Christian by some people, and on the contrary is Christian only up to a certain point. Let me explain. At the Council, I, too, voted for the "Message to the World" of the Council Fathers. In it we said: the principal task of divinizing does not exempt the Church from the task of humanizing. I voted for *Gaudium et Spes*. I was moved and enthusiastic when *Populorum Progressio*[1] came out. I think that the Magisterium of the Church will never sufficiently insist in presenting and recommending the solution of the great problems of freedom, justice, peace, development; and Catholic laity will never fight sufficiently to solve these problems. It is wrong, on the other hand, to state that political, economic and social liberation coincides with salvation in Jesus Christ, that the *Regnum Dei* is identified with the *Regnum hominis*,[2] that *ubi Lenin, ibi Ierusalem*.[3]

7. In the last few days the subject "the future of hope" has been dealt with at Freiburg, on the eighty-fifth *Katholikentag*.[4] They were speaking of the "world" to be improved, and the word "future" was right. But if we pass from hope for the "world" to hope for individual souls, then we must speak also of "eternity". On the seashore at Ostia, in a famous conversation, Augustine and Monica,[5] "forgetting the past and turning to the future, asked themselves what eternal life would be" (*S. Augustini, Confessiones*, IX, 10).[6] This is Christian hope; this is what Pope John intended and what we intend when we pray, with the catechism: "My God, I hope from your goodness... eternal life and the necessary graces to deserve it with good works, which I must do and want to do. My God, let me not remain confounded for ever".[7]

---

[1] The Encyclical Letter on the Development of Peoples "*Populorum Progressio*" was promulgated by Pope Saint Paul VI in 1967; *AAS* 59 [1967], pp. 257-299.

[2] *Regnum Dei* [the Kingdom of God]; *Regnum hominis* [the Kingdom of man].

[3] "*Ubi Lenin, ibi Ierusalem* [Where Lenin is, there is Jerusalem]"; cf. ERNST BLOCH (1885–1977), *Das Prinzip Hoffnung* [*The Principle of Hope*]. Bloch was a German Marxist philosopher and atheist theologian.

[4] *Katholikentag* [Catholic's Day] is a festival-like gathering in German-speaking countries organized by the laity. *Katholikentag* festivals occur approximately every two to four years in Germany, Austria, and Switzerland. The first *Katholikentag* festival was organised by Adam Franz Lennig and held in Mainz from 3 to 6 October 1848.

[5] Saint Monica of Hippo (331-387), mother of Saint Augustine of Hippo, who wrote extensively about her in his *Confessions*. Her feast day is 27 August in the Ordinary Form of the Roman Rite and 4 May in the Extraordinary Form.

[6] "*Conloquebamur ergo soli valde dulciter et, præterita obliviscentes in ea quæ ante sunt extenti, quærebamus inter nos apud præsentem veritatem, quod tu es, qualis futura esset vita æterna sanctorum, quam nec oculus vidit nec auris audivit nec in cor hominis ascendit*" (SANCTUS AUGUSTINUS, *Confessiones*, lib. IX, 10).

[7] *Actus Spei* [Act of Hope]; cf. Appendix, p. 52.

3
The Virtue of Charity

By charity, we love God above all things and our neighbor as ourselves
for love of God. Charity, the form of all the virtues,
"binds everything together in perfect harmony" (Col 3:14).[1]

1. "My God, with all my heart above all things I love You, infinite good and our eternal happiness, and for your sake I love my neighbour as myself and forgive offences received. O Lord, may I love you more and more".[2] This is a very well-known prayer, embellished with biblical phrases. My mother taught it to me. I recite it several times a day even now, and I will try to explain it to you, word by word, as a parish catechist would do.

We are at Pope John's "third lamp of sanctification": charity. *I love*. In philosophy class the teacher would say to me: You know Saint Mark's bell tower? You do? That means that it has somehow, entered your mind: physically it has remained where it was, but within you it has imprinted almost an intellectual portrait of itself. Do you, on the other hand, love Saint Mark's bell tower? That means that portrait, from within, pushes you and bends you, almost carries you, makes you go in your mind towards the bell tower which is outside. In a word: to love means travelling, rushing with one's heart towards the object loved. *The Imitation of Christ*[3] says: he who loves "*currit, volat, laetatur*", runs, flies, and rejoices (*The Imitation of Christ*, 1. III, c. V, n. 4).

To love God is therefore a journeying with one's heart to God. A wonderful journey! When I was a boy, I was thrilled by the journeys described by Jules Verne (*Twenty Thousand Leagues under the Sea, From the Earth to the Moon, Round the World in Eighty Days*, etc).[4] But the journeys of love for God are far more interesting. You read them in the lives of the Saints. Saint Vincent de Paul, whose feast we celebrate today,

---

[1] « *Caritate Deum super omnia et nostrum proximum tamquam nosmetipsos proter amorem diligimus Dei. Ipsa est "vinculum perfectionis" (Colossenses 3,14) et omnium virtutum forma* » (*Catechismus Catholicæ Ecclesiæ*, editio typica 1997, n. 1844).

[2] *Actus Caritatis* [Act of Charity]; cf. Appendix, p. 52.

[3] *The Imitation of Christ* (*De imitatione Christi*) by Thomas à Kempis (1380-1471) was first published anonymously in Latin *circa* 1418 and is considered one of the greatest manuals of devotion in all of Christianity.

[4] Jules Gabriel Verne (1828-1905) was a French novelist, poet, and playwright. He is best known for his adventure novels and his profound influence on the literary genre of science fiction. His notable works include: *Twenty Thousand Leagues under the Sea, Journey to the Centre of the Earth, Around the World in Eighty Days*, and *The Mysterious Island*.

for example, is a giant of charity: he loved God more than a father and a mother, and he himself was a father for prisoners, sick people, orphans and the poor. Saint Peter Claver,[1] dedicating himself entirely to God, used to sign: *Peter, the slave of the Ethiopians for ever*.[2]

The Journey also brings sacrifices, but these must not stop us. Jesus is on the cross: you want to kiss him? You cannot help bending over the cross and letting yourself be pricked by some thorns of the crown which is on the Lord's head (cf. St Francis de Sales, *Œuvres*, éd. Annecy, t. XXI, p. 153). You cannot cut the figure of good Saint Peter, who had no difficulty in shouting "Long live Jesus" on Mount Tabor, where there was joy, but did not even let himself be seen beside Jesus at Mount Calvary, where there was risk and suffering (cf. *ibid.*, t. XV, p. 140).

Love for God is also a mysterious journey: that is, I cannot start unless God takes the initiative first. "No one", Jesus said, "can come to me, unless the Father who sent me draws him" (*Jn* 6:44).[3] Saint Augustine asked himself: but what about human freedom? God, however, who willed and constructed this freedom, knows how to respect it, though bringing hearts to the point he intended: *"parum est voluntate, etiam voluptate traheris"*; God draws you not only in a way that you yourself want, but even in such a way that you enjoy being drawn (*S. Augustini, In Io. Evang. tract.* [*Tractates on the Gospel of John*], 26, 44).[4]

With all my heart. I stress, here, the adjective "all". Totalitarianism, in politics, is an ugly thing. In religion, on the contrary, a totalitarianism on our side towards God is a very good thing. It is written:

> You shall love the LORD your God with all your heart, and with all your soul, and with all your might. And these words which I command you this day shall be upon your heart; and you shall teach them diligently to your children, and shall talk of them when you sit in your house, and when you walk by the way, and when you lie down, and when you rise. And you shall bind them as a sign upon your hand, and they shall be as frontlets between your eyes. And you

---

[1] Saint Peter Claver Corberó (1581-1654) was a Spanish missionary priest and a member of the Society of Jesus (Jesuits). The patron saint of slaves, the Republic of Colombia, and ministry to African Americans, he was beatified in 1851 by Blessed Pius IX and canonised in 1888 by Pope Leo XIII. His feast day is 9 September.
[2] *"Petrus Claver, æthiopum semper servus* [Peter Claver, servant of the Ethiopians forever]".
[3] *"Nemo potest venire ad me, nisi Pater, qui misit me, traxerit eum"* (*Ioannem* 6, 44).
[4] SANCTUS AUGUSTINUS, *In Evangelium Joannis Tractatus* CXXIV: *PL* 35 1379-1976

shall write them on the doorposts of your house and on your gates (*Dt* 6:5-9).[1]

That "all" repeated and applied insistently is really the banner of Christian maximalism. And it is right: God is too great, he deserves too much from us for us to be able to throw to him, as to a poor Lazarus,[2] a few crumbs of our time and our heart. He is infinite good and will be our eternal happiness: money, pleasure, the fortunes of this world, compared with him, are just fragments of good and fleeting moments of happiness. It would not be wise to give so much of ourselves to these things and little of ourselves to Jesus.

Above everything else. Now we come to a direct comparison between God and man, between God and the world. It would not be right to say: "Either God or man". We must love "both God and man"; the latter, however, never more than God or against God or as much as God. In other words: love of God, though prevalent, is not exclusive. The Bible declares Jacob holy (*Dn* 3:35) and loved by God (*Mal* 1:2; *Rom* 9:13), it shows him working for seven years to win Rachel as his wife; "and they seemed to him but a few days because of the love he had for her" (*Gen* 29:20).[3] Francis de Sales makes a little comment on these words: "Jacob", he writes, "loves Rachel with all his might, and he loves God with all his might; but he does not therefore love Rachel as God nor God as Rachel. He loves God as his God above all things and more than himself; he loves Rachel as his wife above all other women and as himself. He loves God with absolutely and superbly supreme love, and Rachel with supreme husbandly love; one love is not contrary to the other because love of Rachel does not violate the supreme advantages of love of God" (St Francis de Sales, *Œuvres*, éd. Annecy, t. V, p. 175).

And for your sake I love my neighbour. Here we are in the presence of two loves which are "twin brothers" and inseparable. It is easy to love some persons; difficult to love others; we do not find them likeable, they have offended us and hurt us; only if I love God in earnest can I love them as sons of God and because he asks me to. Jesus also established

---
[1] "*Diliges Dominum Deum tuum ex toto corde tuo et ex tota anima tua et ex tota fortitudine tua. Eruntque verba hæc, quæ ego praecipio tibi hodie, in corde tuo, et inculcabis ea filiis tuis et loqueris ea sedens in domo tua et ambulans in itinere, decumbens atque consurgens; et ligabis ea quasi signum in manu tua, eruntque quasi appensum quid inter oculos tuos, scribesque ea in postibus domus tuæ et in portis tuis*" (*Deuteronomii* 6, 5-9).
[2] Cf. *Luke* 16:19-31.
[3] "*Et videbantur illi pauci dies præ amoris magnitudine*" (*Genesis* 29, 20).

how to love one's neighbour: that is, not only with feeling, but with facts. This is the way, he said. I will ask you: I was hungry in the person of my humbler brothers, did you give me food? Did you visit me, when I was sick (cf. *Mt* 25:34ff).

2. The catechism puts these and other words of the Bible in the double list of the seven corporal works of mercy and the seven spiritual ones. The list is not complete and it would be necessary to update it. Among the starving, for example, today, it is no longer a question just of this or that individual; there are whole peoples.

3. We all remember the great words of Pope Paul VI:

> Today the peoples in hunger are making a dramatic appeal to the peoples blessed with abundance. The Church shudders at this cry of anguish and calls each one to give a loving response of charity to this brother's cry for help (*Populorum Progressio*, 3).[1]

At this point justice is added to charity, because, Paul VI says also:

> Private property does not constitute for anyone an absolute and unconditioned right. No one is justified in keeping for his exclusive use what he does not need, when others lack necessities (*Populorum Progressio*, 23).[2]

Consequently "every exhausting armaments race becomes an intolerable scandal" (*Populorum Progressio*, 53).[3]

4. In the light of these strong expressions it can be seen how far we—individuals and peoples—still are from loving others "as ourselves", as Jesus commanded.

---

[1] "*Fame laborantes populi hodie divitiis præpollentes populos miserabili quadam voce compellant. Quapropter Ecclesia, anxiis huiusmodi clamoribus quodammodo cohorrescens, singulos omnes vocat, ut amore impulsi quasi fratribus opem implorantibus tandem suas dedant aures*" (SANCTUS PAULUS VI, Litt. enc. *Populorum Progressio*, 3: *AAS* 59 (1967), p. 258).

[2] "*Privatam bonorum proprietatem nemini ius tale concedere, quod supremum sit nullique condicioni obnoxium. Nemini licet bona, quæ sibi superent, unire ad privata commoda seponere, cum alii rebus careant vitæ necessariis*" (SANCTUS PAULUS VI, Litteræ encyclicæ *Populorum Progressio*, 23: *AAS* 59 (1967), p. 269).

[3] "*Quævis denique exinaniens ad congerenda arma certatio: hæc omnia, dicimus, in famosum intolerandumque flagitium transeunt*" (IBID., n. 59: p. 286).

5. Another commandment: *I forgive offences received.* It almost seems that the Lord gives precedence to this forgiveness over worship:

> So if you are offering your gift at the altar, and there remember that your brother has something against you, leave your gift there before the altar and go; first be reconciled to your brother, and then come and offer your gift (*Mt* 5:23-24).[1]

6. The last words of the prayer are: *Lord, may I love you more and more.* Here, too, there is obedience to a commandment of God, who put thirst for progress in our hearts. From pile-dwellings, caves and the first huts we have passed to houses, apartment buildings and skyscrapers; from journeys on foot, on the back of a mule or of a camel, to coaches, trains and aeroplanes. And people desire to progress further with more and more rapid means of transport, reaching more and more distant goals. But to love God, we have seen, is also a journey: God wants it to be more and more intense and perfect. He said to all his followers: "You are the light of the world, the salt of the earth" (*Mt* 5:13-14);[2] "You, therefore, must be perfect, as your heavenly Father is perfect" (*Mt* 5:48).[3] That means: to love God not a little, but so much; not to stop at the point at which we have arrived, but with his help, to progress in love.

Blessed John Paul I
27 September 1978

---

[1] "*Si ergo offeres munus tuum ad altare, et ibi recordatus fueris quia frater tuus habet aliquid adversum te, relinque ibi munus tuum ante altare et vade, prius, reconciliare fratri tuo et tunc veniens offer munus tuum*" (*Matthæum* 5, 23-24).

[2] "*Vos estis lux mundi*" (*Matthæum* 5, 14).

[3] "*Estote ergo vos perfecti, sicut Pater vester cælestis perfectus est*" (*Matthæum* 5, 48).

Part II
The Cardinal Virtues

Pope Saint John Paul II

4
The Virtue of Prudence

Prudence disposes the practical reason to discern, in every circumstance, our true good and to choose the right means for achieving it.[1]

1. When the Holy Father John Paul I spoke to participants in the General Audience on Wednesday 27 September, no one could imagine that it was for the last time. His death—after thirty-three days of pontificate—surprised the whole world and filled it with a deep sense of loss. He who brought forth such great joy in the Church and inspired such hope in men's hearts, consummated and terminated his mission, in such a short time. In his death the words so often repeated in the Gospel came true: "…be ready; for the Son of man is coming at an hour you do not expect" (*Mt* 24:44).[2] John Paul I always kept watch. The Lord's call did not take him by surprise. He followed it with the same trembling joy with which he had accepted the election to Saint Peter's throne on 26 August.

2. Today John Paul II presents himself to you, for the first time. Four weeks after that General Audience, he wishes to greet you and speak to you. He wishes to carry on with the subjects already started by John Paul I. We remember that he spoke of the three theological virtues: faith, hope and charity. He ended with charity. As Saint Paul teaches (*1 Cor* 13:13), charity—which constituted his last teaching—is the greatest virtue here on earth; it is the one that crosses the threshold of life and death. For when the time of faith and hope ends, love continues. John Paul I has already passed through the time of faith, hope, and charity, charity which has been expressed so magnificently on this earth, and the fullness of which is revealed only in eternity.

3. Today we must speak of another virtue, since I have learned from the notes of the late Pontiff that it was his intention to speak not only of the three theological virtues, faith, hope and charity, but also of the four so-called cardinal virtues. John Paul I wished to speak of the "seven lamps" of the Christian life, as Pope John XXIII called them.

---

[1] « *Prudentia practicam disponit rationem ad nostrum verum bonum discernendum in omnibus adiunctis et ad iusta seligenda media ad illud adimplendum* » (*Catechismus Catholicæ Ecclesiæ*, editio typica 1997, n. 1835).

[2] "*Ideo et vos estote parati, quia, qua nescitis hora, Filius hominis venturus est*" (*Matthæum* 24, 44).

4. Well, today I wish to continue this plan, which the late Pope had prepared, and to speak briefly of the virtue of prudence. The ancients[1] spoke a great deal of this virtue. We owe them, for this reason, deep gratitude and thanks. In a certain dimension, they taught us that the value of man must be measured with the yardstick of the moral good which he accomplishes in his life. It is just this that ensures the virtue of prudence in the first place. The prudent man, who strives for everything that is really good, endeavours to measure everything, every situation and his whole activity according to the yardstick of moral good. So a prudent man is not one who—as is often meant—is able to wangle things in life and draw the greatest profit from it; but one who is able to construct his whole life according to the voice of upright conscience and according to the requirements of sound morality.

5. So prudence is the key for the accomplishment of the fundamental task that each of us has received from God. This task is the perfection of man himself. God has given our humanity to each of us. We must meet this task by planning it accordingly.

6. But the Christian has the right and the duty to look at the virtue of prudence also in another perspective. It is, as it were, the image and likeness of the Providence of God himself in the dimensions of concrete man. For man—as we know from the book of Genesis—was created in the image and likeness of God. And God carries out his plan in the history of creation, and above all in the history of mankind. The purpose of this plan is—as Saint Thomas teaches—the ultimate good of the universe. The same plan in the history of mankind becomes simply the plan of salvation, the plan that embraces us all. At the central point of its realisation is Jesus Christ, in whom was expressed the eternal love and solicitude of God himself, the Father, for the salvation of man. This is at the same time the full expression of Divine Providence.

7. Well, man who is the image of God, must—as Saint Thomas again teaches—in some way be providence: but within the proportions of his life. He can take part in this great march of all creatures towards the purpose, which is the good of creation. He must—expressing ourselves even more in the language of faith—take part in the divine plan of salvation. He must march towards salvation, and help others to save themselves. By helping others, he saves himself.

---

[3] Classical antiquity (ancient Greece and ancient Rome); 800 BC – 1000 AD.

8. I pray in order that, in this light, those who are listening to me will think now of their own lives. Am I prudent? Do I live consistently and responsibly? Does the programme I am realising serve the true good? Does it serve the salvation that Christ and the Church want for us? If a boy or girl student, a son or a daughter, is listening to me today, let such a person look in this light at the homework, reading, interests, pastimes, the circle of friends, boys and girls. If a father or a mother of a family is listening to me, let such a person think a little of the conjugal and parental commitments. If a minister or statesman is listening to me, let him look at the range of his duties and responsibilities. Is he pursuing the real good of society, of the nation, of mankind? Or only particular and partial interests? If a journalist or publicist is listening to me, one who exercises an influence on public opinion, let such a person reflect on the value and purpose of this influence.

9. I, too, who am speaking to you, I the Pope, what must I do to act prudently? There comes into my mind the letters[1] to Saint Bernard[2] of Albino Luciani, then Patriarch of Venice. In his answer to Cardinal Luciani, the Abbot of Chiaravalle—a Doctor of the Church—recalls emphatically that he who governs must be "prudent". What, then, must the new Pope do in order to operate prudently? Certainly he must do a great deal in this direction. He must always learn and always meditate on these problems. But in addition to this, what can he do? He must pray and endeavour to have that gift of the Holy Spirit which is called the gift of counsel. And let all those who wish the new Pope to be a prudent Pastor of the Church, implore for him the gift of counsel.[3] And for themselves, let them also ask for this gift through the special intercession of the Mother of Good Counsel.[4] For it ought to be very greatly desired that all men will behave prudently and that those who wield power will act with true prudence.

---

[1] When he was the Patriarch of Venice, the Venerable Pope John Paul I wrote a series of letters to a wide collection of historical and fictional persons, including Christ Jesus, King David, Mark Twain, Charles Dickens, Figaro the Barber, Empress Maria Theresa, and Pinocchio. They were originally published in the Italian Christian paper *Messaggero di S. Antonio* between 1972 and 1975. They were published in book form in 1976 under the title *Illustrissimi* [*To the Illustrious Ones*]. Upon his election to the See of Peter in 1978, the work was translated into English and published after his death.

[2] Saint Bernard of Clairvaux (1090-1153) was a French Cistercian abbot and spiritual writer and is a Doctor of the Church. His feast day is 20 August.

[3] Cf. *Isaiah* 11:1-2.

[4] *Mater boni consilii* (*Litaniæ Lauretanæ*).

So may the Church—prudently strengthening herself with the gifts of the Holy Spirit and, in particular, with the gift of counsel—take part effectively in this great march towards the good of all, and so may she show to everyone the way to eternal salvation.

Saint John Paul II
25 October 1978

5
The Virtue of Justice

*Justice consists in the firm and constant will
to give God and neighbour their due.*[1]

1. During these first audiences in which I have the fortune to meet you, who come here from Rome, Italy, and from so many other countries, I wish, as I said already on 25 October, to continue to develop the subjects chosen by John Paul I, my Predecessor. He wished to speak not only of the three theological virtues: faith, hope and charity, but also of the four cardinal virtues: prudence, justice, fortitude and temperance. He saw in them—all together—seven lamps, as it were, of sanctification. God called him to eternity, and he was able to speak only of the three principal ones: faith, hope and charity, which illuminate the Christian's whole life. His unworthy Successor, in meeting with you to reflect, in the spirit of his late Predecessor, on the cardinal virtues, wishes to light, in a certain sense, the other lamps at his tomb.

2. Today, it falls to me to speak of justice. It is perhaps well that this should be the subject of the first catechesis in the month of November. This month, in fact, induces us to fix our gaze on the life of every man, and at the same time on the life of the whole of mankind, in the perspective of final justice. We are all aware, somehow, that in this transitory world, it is not possible to achieve the full measure of justice. The words so often heard: "There is no justice in this world" are, perhaps, the fruit of an oversimplification that is too facile. But they contain a principle of deep truth all the same. Justice is, in a certain way, greater than man, than the dimensions of his earthly life, than the possibilities of establishing in this life fully just relations among men, environments, societies and social groups, nations, and so on. Every man lives and dies with a certain sense of an insatiable hunger for justice, since the world is not able to satisfy fully a being created in the image of God, either in the depths of his person or in the various aspects of his human life. And thus, by means of this hunger for justice, man turns to God who "is justice itself". Jesus expressed this very clearly and concisely in the Sermon on the Mount, when he said: "Blessed are those who hunger and thirst for righteousness, for they shall be satisfied" (*Mt* 5:6).[2]

---

[1] « *Iustitia in constanti et firma consistit voluntate Deo et proximo tribuendi id, quod illis debetur* » (*Catechismus Catholicæ Ecclesiæ*, editio typica 1997, n. 1836).
[2] "*Beati, qui esuriunt et sitiunt iustitiam, quoniam ipsi saturabuntur*" (*Matthæum* 5, 6).

3. Having this evangelical sense of justice before our eyes, we must consider it at the same time a fundamental dimension of man's life on earth: the life of man, of society, of humanity. This is the ethical dimension. Justice is the fundamental principle of the existence and the coexistence of men, as well as of human communities, societies and peoples. Furthermore, justice is the principle of the existence of the Church, as the People of God, and the principle of coexistence of the Church and the various social structures; in particular of the state, as well as of international organizations. In this wide and differentiated area, man and mankind are continually seeking justice: this is a perennial process and it is a task of supreme importance.

According to the different relationships and different aspects, justice has obtained more appropriate definitions throughout the centuries. Hence the concept of justice: communicative, distributive, legal and social. All this testifies what a fundamental significance justice has for the moral order among men, in social and international relations. It can be said that the very meaning of man's existence on earth is bound up with justice. To define correctly "how much is due" to each one from all and at the same time to all from each one, "what is due" (*debitum*) to man from man in different systems and relationships—to define, and above all to put into practice!—is a great thing, through which every man lives, and thanks to which his life has a meaning.

Therefore there remains, during the centuries of human existence on earth, a continual effort and a continuous struggle to organize in accordance with justice the whole of social life in its various aspects. It is necessary to view with respect the multiple programmes and the activity, sometimes reformative, of various trends and systems. It is necessary, at the same time, to be aware that here it is not a question in the first place of systems, but of justice and of man. The system must be for man, not man for the system.

Therefore defence is necessary against the hardening of the system. I am thinking of social, economic, political, and cultural systems, which must be sensitive to man, to his complete good. They must be able to reform themselves, their own structures, according to what the full truth about man requires. The great effort of our times, which aims at defining and consolidating "human rights" in the life of present-day mankind, peoples, and states, must be evaluated from this point of view.

The Church of our century remains in continual dialogue on the great front of the modern world, as is testified to by many encyclicals of the Popes and the doctrine of the Second Vatican Council. The present Pope will certainly have to return repeatedly to these matters. In today's brief exposition, all that can be done is to draw attention to this vast and differentiated area.

4. Each of us, then, must be able to live in a context of justice and, even more, each of us must be just and act justly with regard to those near us and those who are far away, with regard to the community, to the society of which one is a member… and with regard to God.

Justice has many references and many forms. There is also a form of justice which regards what man "owes" God. This is a vast subject in itself. I will not develop it now, although I cannot abstain from indicating it.

Let us give our attention, meanwhile, to men. Christ left us the commandment to love our neighbour. In this commandment, everything that concerns justice is also contained. There can be no love without justice. Love "surpasses" justice, but at the same time it finds its verification in justice. Even a father and a mother, loving their own child, must be just in his regard. If justice is uncertain, love, too, runs a risk.

To be just means giving each one what is due to him. This concerns temporal goods, of a material nature. The best example here can be remuneration for work or the so-called right to the fruits of one's own work or of one's own land. But to man is due also his good name, respect, consideration, the reputation he has deserved. The more we know a man, the more his personality, his character, his intellect and his heart are revealed to us. And the more we realize—and we must realise!—with what criterion to "measure him" and what it means to be just towards him.

It is necessary, therefore, to deepen our knowledge of justice continually. It is not a theoretical science. It is virtue, it is capacity of the human spirit, of the human will and also of the heart. It is also necessary to pray in order to be just and to know how to be just.

We cannot forget our Lord's words: "The measure you give will be the measure you get" (*Matthew* 7:2).[1]

A just man is a man of a "just measure".
May we all be so!
May we all strive constantly to become so!
My blessing to all.

Saint John Paul II
8 November 1978

---

[1] "*In qua mensura mensi fueritis, metietur vobis*" (*Matthæum* 7, 2).

6
The Virtue of Fortitude

Fortitude ensures firmness in difficulties
and constancy in the pursuit of the good.[1]

1. Speaking from the loggia of Saint Peter's Basilica, on the day after his election, Pope John Paul I recalled, among other things, that during the Conclave on 26 August, when everything already seemed to indicate that he himself would be chosen, the Cardinals beside him whispered in his ear: "Courage!" Probably this word was necessary for him at that moment and had been imprinted on his heart, since he recalled it immediately the next day.

   John Paul I will forgive me if I use this story of his now. I think it can better introduce all of us present here to the subject which I intend to develop. I wish, in fact, to speak today of the third cardinal virtue, that of fortitude. It is precisely to this virtue that we refer, when we wish to exhort someone to be courageous, as John Paul's neighbour did at the Conclave, when he said to him: "Courage".

2. Whom do we regard as a strong, courageous man? This word usually conjures up the soldier who defends his homeland, exposing to danger his health, and in wartime, even his life. We realize, however, that we need fortitude also in peacetime. And so we highly esteem persons who distinguish themselves for so-called "civil courage". A testimony of fortitude is offered to us by anyone who risks his own life to save someone who is about to drown, or by one who provides help in natural calamities, such as fire, floods, etc. Saint Charles, my patron saint,[2] certainly distinguished himself for this virtue when, during the plague in Milan, he carried out his pastoral ministry among the inhabitants of that city. But we think also with admiration of those men who climb the peaks of Everest[3] or

---

[1] « *Fortitudo firmitatem in difficultatibus præbet et constantiam in bono prosequendo* » (*Catechismus Catholicæ Ecclesiæ*, editio typica 1997, n. 1837).

[2] Saint Charles of Borromeo (Italian: *Carlo Borromeo*; Latin: *Carolus Borromeus*) (1538-1584) was one of the great reformers of the sixteenth century, taking part in the Council of Trent (1545–1563) and playing a large role in the creation of *The Roman Catechism* (*Catechismus Romanus*). He was elevated to the Sacred College of Cardinals in 1560 by his uncle, Pope Pius IV, and appointed 15th Archbishop of Milan in 1564. He was beatified in 1602 and canonised in 1610 by Pope Paul V. His feast day is 4 November.

[3] Mount Everest is the highest mountain on earth, with a peak measured at 8,848 metres (29,029 feet) above sea level. It is the fifth tallest mountain measured from the centre of the earth. Mount Everest is located in the Mahalangur section of the Himalayas in Asia.

of the cosmonauts who set foot on the moon for the first time.[1]

3. As can be seen from all this, the manifestations of the virtue of fortitude are numerous. Some of them are well known and enjoy a certain fame. Others are less known, although they often call for even greater virtue. Fortitude, in fact, as we said at the beginning, is a virtue, a cardinal virtue. Allow me to draw your attention to examples that are generally not well known, but which bear witness in themselves to great, sometimes even heroic, virtue. I am thinking, for example, of a woman, already mother of a large family, who is "advised" by so many to suppress a new life conceived in her womb, by undergoing "the operation" of interruption of pregnancy; and she replies firmly: "no". She certainly feels all the difficulty that this "no" brings with it, difficulty for herself, for her husband, for the whole family, and yet she replies: "no". The new human life conceived in her is a value too great, too "sacred", for her to be able to give in to such pressure.

4. Another example: a man who is promised freedom and also an easy career provided he denies his own principles, or approves of something that is against his sense of honesty towards others. And he, too, replies "no", though faced by threats on the one side, and attractions on the other. Here we have a courageous man!

5. There are many, a great many manifestations of fortitude, often heroic, of which nothing is written in the newspapers, or of which little is known. Only human conscience knows them… and God knows!

6. I wish to pay tribute to all these unknown courageous people. To all those who have the courage to say "no" or "yes", when they have to pay a price to do so! To the men who bear an extraordinary witness to human dignity and deep humanity. Just because they are unknown, they deserve a tribute and special recognition.

7. According to the teaching of Saint Thomas, the virtue of fortitude is found in the man,
   — who is ready "*aggredi pericula*", that is, to face danger;
   — who is ready "*sustinere mala*", that is, to put up with adversities for a just cause, for truth, for justice, etc.

---

[1] The original Italian text uses the term *cosmonauti* (cosmonauts). English-speaking countries generally use the term astronaut. Both words have their origins in Greek. The first man-made object to reach the surface of the Moon was the Soviet Union's Luna 2 mission on 13 September 1959. The first manned mission to land on the Moon was the United States' Apollo 11 on 20 July 1969.

8. The virtue of fortitude always calls for a certain overcoming of human weakness and particularly of fear. Man, indeed, by nature, spontaneously fears danger, affliction and suffering. Therefore courageous men must be sought not only on battlefields, but also in hospital wards or on a bed of pain. Such men could often be found in concentration camps or in places of deportation. They were real heroes.

9. Fear sometimes deprives of civil courage men who are living in a climate of threats, oppression or persecution. The men who are capable of crossing the so-called barrier of fear, to bear witness to truth and justice, have then a special value. To reach such fortitude, man must in a certain way "go beyond" his own limits and "transcend" himself, running "the risk" of an unknown situation, the risk of being frowned upon, the risk of laying himself open to unpleasant consequences, insults, degradations, material losses, perhaps imprisonment or persecution. To attain this fortitude, man must be sustained by a great love for truth and for good, to which he dedicates himself.

The virtue of fortitude proceeds hand in hand with the capacity of sacrificing oneself. This virtue had already a well-defined contour among the Ancients. With Christ it acquired an evangelical, Christian contour. The Gospel is addressed to weak, poor, meek and humble men, peacemakers and to the merciful, but, at the same time, it contains a constant appeal to fortitude. It often repeats: "Have no fear" (*Mt* 14:27).[1] It teaches man that, for a just cause, for truth, for justice, one must be able to "lay down one's life" (*Jn* 15:13).[2]

10. I wish here to refer to yet another example, which goes back 400 years ago, but which still remains alive and relevant today. It is the case of Saint Stanislaus Kostka,[3] the patron saint of the young, whose tomb is in the church of *Sant'Andrea al Quirinale*, in Rome.[4] Here, in fact, he ended his life at the age of eighteen. By nature he was very sensitive and tender,

---

[1] "*Nolite timere*" (*Matthæum* 14, 27).
[2] "*Maiorem hac dilectionem nemo habet, ut animam suam quis ponat pro amicis suis*" (*Io* 15, 13); "Greater love has no man than this, that a man lay down his life for his friends" (*RSV-2CE*).
[3] Saint Stanislaus (Stanisław) Kostka was born at Rostkowo in Poland on 28 October 1550. On his 17th birthday in 1567, he entered the Society of Jesus (Jesuits) in Rome. Less than a year later, he died on 15 August 1568. He was beatified in 1605 and canonised on 31 December 1726. His feast day is 13 November.
[4] The Church of Saint Andrew's at the Quirinal (Italian: *Sant'Andrea al Quirinale*; Latin: *S. Andreæ in Quirinali*) is one of the titular churches of Rome assigned a cardinal-priest. Construction began in 1658 and was completed in 1670.

yet very courageous. Fortitude led him, coming from a noble family, to choose to be poor, following the example of Christ, and to put himself in his exclusive service. Although his decision met with firm oppositio on the part of his circle, he succeeded with great love, but also with great firmness, in realizing his resolution, contained in the motto: "*Ad maiora natus sum*" ("I was born for greater things"). He arrived at the novitiate of the Jesuits, travelling from Vienna to Rome on foot and trying to escape from his pursuers who wished by force to turn this "obstinate" youth from his intentions.

11. I know that in the month of November many young people from all over Rome, and especially students, pupils and novices, visit the tomb of Saint Stanislaus in Saint Andrew's church. I am together with them, because our generation, too, needs men who can repeat with holy "obstinacy": "*Ad maiora natus sum*". We need strong men!

12. To be men we need fortitude. The truly prudent man, in fact, is only he who possesses the virtue of fortitude; just as also the truly just man is only he who has the virtue of fortitude.

13. Let us pray for this gift of the Holy Spirit which is called the "gift of fortitude".[1] When man lacks the strength to "transcend" himself, in view of higher values, such as truth, justice, vocation, faithfulness in marriage, this "gift from above" must make each of us a strong man and, at the right moment, say to us "deep down": Courage!

Saint John Paul II
15 November 1978

---

[2] Cf. *Isaiah* 11:1-2.

7
The Virtue of Temperance

Temperance moderates the attraction of the pleasures of the senses and provides balance in the use of created goods.[1]

1. In the course of the audiences of my pontifical ministry I have tried to carry out the "testament" of my beloved Predecessor John Paul I. As is known, he did not leave a written testament, because death took him unexpectedly and suddenly, but he left some notes which showed that he had intended, at the first Wednesday meetings, to speak of the fundamental principles of Christian life. That is, he had intended to speak of the three theological virtues (he had time to do this) and then of the four cardinal virtues, (this is being done by his unworthy Successor). Today the turn has come to speak of the fourth cardinal virtue, "temperance", thus completing, in some way, John Paul I's programme, in which we can see the testament, as it were, of the late Pope.

2. When we speak of virtues—not only these cardinal ones, but all of them, every virtue—we must always have in mind the real man, the actual man. Virtue is not something abstract, detached from life, but, on the contrary, it has deep "roots" in life itself, it springs from the latter and forms it. Virtue has an impact on man's life, on his actions and behaviour. It follows that, in all these reflections of ours, we are speaking not so much of the virtue as of man living and acting "virtuously"; we are speaking of the prudent, just and courageous man, and finally, precisely today, we are speaking of the "temperate" (or "sober") man.

   Let us add at once that all these attributes, or rather attitudes of man, coming from the single cardinal virtues, are connected with one another. So it is not possible to be a really prudent, man, or an authentically just one, or a truly strong one, unless one also has the virtue of temperance. It can be said that this virtue indirectly conditions all other virtues, but it must also be said that all the other virtues are indispensable for man to be "temperate" (or "sober").

3. The term "temperance" itself seems in a certain way to refer to what is "outside man". We say, in fact, that a temperate man is one who does not abuse food, drinks, pleasures, who does not drink alcohol to excess, who

---

[1] « *Temperantia allectationem moderatur voluptatum sensibilium atque in bonorum creatorum usu præbet æquilibrium* » (*Catechismus Catholicæ Ecclesiæ*, editio typica 1997, n. 1838).

does not deprive himself of consciousness by the use of drugs, etc. This reference to elements external to man has its basis, however, within man. It is as if there existed in each of us a "higher self" and a "lower self". In our "lower self", our "body" and everything that belongs to it is expressed: its needs, its desires, its passions of a sensual nature particularly. The virtue of temperance guarantees every man mastery of the "lower self" by the "higher self". Is this a humiliation of our body? Or a disability? On the contrary, this mastery gives higher value to the body. As a result of the virtue of temperance, the body and our senses find the right place which pertains to them in our human condition.

A temperate man is one who is master of himself. One in whom passions do not prevail over reason, will, and even the "heart". A man who can control himself! If this is so, we can easily realize what a fundamental and radical value the virtue of temperance has. It is even indispensable, in order that man may be fully a man. It is enough to look at someone who, carried away by his passions, becomes a "victim" of them—renouncing of his own accord the use of reason (such as, for example, an alcoholic, a drug addict)—to see clearly that "to be a man" means respecting one's own dignity, and therefore, among other things, letting oneself be guided by the virtue of temperance.

4. This virtue is also called "sobriety". And rightly so! In fact, to be able to control our passions, the lust of the flesh, the explosions of sensuality (for example in relations with the other sex) etc., we must not go beyond the rightful limit with regard to ourselves and our "lower self". If we do not respect this rightful limit, we will not be able to control ourselves. This does not mean that the virtuous, sober man cannot be "spontaneous", cannot enjoy, cannot weep, cannot express his feelings; that is, it does not mean that he must become insensitive, "indifferent", as if he were made of ice or stone. No, not at all! It is enough to look at Jesus to be convinced of this. Christian morality has never been identified Stoic morality. On the contrary, considering all the riches of affections and emotivity with which every man is endowed—each in a different way, moreover: man in one way, woman in another owing to her own sensitivity—it must be recognised that man cannot reach this mature spontaneity unless by means of continuous work on himself and special "vigilance" over his whole behaviour. The virtue of "temperance", of "sobriety" consists, in fact in this.

5. I think, too, that this virtue demands from each of us a specific humility with regard to the gifts that God has put in our human nature. I would say "humility of the body" and that "of the heart". This humility is a necessary condition for man's interior "harmony": for man's "interior" beauty. Let everyone think it over carefully; and in particular young men, and even more young women, at the age when one is so anxious to be handsome or beautiful in order to please others! Let us remember that man must above all be beautiful interiorly. Without this beauty, all efforts aimed at the body alone will not make—either him or her—a really beautiful person.

Is it not just the body, moreover, that undergoes considerable and often even serious damage to health, if man lacks the virtue of temperance, of sobriety? In this connection, the statistics and files of hospitals all over the world, could say a great deal. Also doctors who work on the advisory bureaus to which married couples, fiancés and young people apply, have great experience of this. It is true that we cannot judge virtue on the exclusive basis of the criterion of psychophysical health; there are many proofs, however, that the lack of the virtue, of temperance, sobriety, damages health.

6. I must end here, although I am convinced that this subject is interrupted rather than exhausted. Perhaps there will be an opportunity one day to return to it. For the present this is enough.

I have tried in this way, as well as I could, to follow John Paul I's testament. I ask him to pray for me, when I shall have to pass to other topics during the Wednesday audiences.[1]

Saint John Paul II
22 November 1978

---

[1] The catechetical series of Pope Saint John Paul II include: Catechesis on the Book of Genesis, popularly known as the "Theology of the Body" (1979-1984); Catechesis on the Creed (1985-1995); Catechesis on the Blessed Virgin Mary (1995-1997), Catechesis on the History of Salvation (1997-2001); Catechesis on the Psalms and Canticles of Lauds and Vespers (2001-2005)

Appendices

I
Prayers for the Seven Virtues in Latin and English

Actus virtutum theologalium[1]

ACTUS FIDE
Dómine Deus, firma fide credo et confíteor ómnia et síngula quæ sancta Ecclésia Cathólica propónit, quia tu, Deus, ea omnia revelásti, qui es ætérna véritas et sapiéntia quæ nec fállere nec falli potest.
In hac fide vívere et mori státuo.
Amen.

ACTUS SPEI
Dómine Deus, spero per grátiam tuam remissiónem ómnium peccatórum, et post hanc vitam ætérnam felicitátem me esse consecutúrum: quia tu promisísti, qui es infiníte potens, fidélis, benígnus, et miséricors.
In hac spe vívere et mori státuo.
Amen.

ACTUS CARITATIS
Dómine Deus, amo te super ómnia próximum meum propter te, quia tu es summum, infinítum, et perfectíssimum bonum, omni dilectióne dignum.
In hac caritáte vívere et mori státuo.
Amen.

Acts of the Theological Virtues

ACT OF FAITH
O my God, I firmly believe that you are one God in three divine Persons, Father, Son, and Holy Spirit. I believe that your divine Son became man and died for our sins and that he will come to judge the living and the dead. I believe these and all the truths which the Holy Catholic Church teaches because you have revealed them who are eternal truth and wisdom, who can neither deceive nor be deceived.
In this faith I intend to live and die.
Amen.

ACT OF HOPE
O Lord God, I hope by your grace for the pardon of all my sins and after life here to gain eternal happiness because you have promised it who are infinitely powerful, faithful, kind, and merciful.
In this hope I intend to live and die.
Amen.

ACT OF CHARITY OR LOVE
O Lord God, I love you above all things and I love my neighbor for your sake because you are the highest, infinite and perfect good, worthy of all my love.
In this love I intend to live and die.
Amen.

---

[1] *Compendium of the Catechism of the Catholic Church*, 2006: Appendix of Common Prayers.

II
A Prayer to Acquire the Virtues
by Saint Thomas Aquinas[1]

O God, all-powerful and all-knowing, without beginning and without end, you who are the source, the sustainer, and the rewarder of all virtues, grant that I may abide on the firm ground of faith, be sheltered by an impregnable shield of hope, and be adorned in the bridal garment of charity.

Grant that I may through justice be subject to you, through prudence avoid the beguilements of the devil, through temperance exercise restraint, and through fortitude endure adversity with patience.

Grant that whatever good things I have, I may share generously with those who have not and that whatever good things I do not have, I may request humbly from those who do.

Grant that I may judge rightly the evil of the wrongs that I have done and bear calmly the punishments I have brought upon myself, and that I may never envy my neighbour's possessions and ever give thanks for your good things.

Grant that I may always observe modesty in the way I dress, the way I walk, and the gestures I use, restrain my tongue from frivolous talk, prevent my feet from leading me astray, keep my eyes from wandering glances, shelter my ears from rumours, lower my gaze in humility, lift my mind to thoughts of heaven, condemn all that will pass away, and love you only.

Grant that I may subdue my flesh and cleanse my conscience, honour the saints and praise you worthily, advance in goodness, and end a life of good works with a holy death.

Plant deep in me, Lord, all the virtues, that I might be devout in divine matters, discerning in human affairs, and burdensome to no one in fulfilling my own bodily needs.

Grant to me, Lord, fervent contrition, pure confession, and complete reparation. Order me inwardly through a good life that I might do what is right and what will be meritorious for me and a good example for others.

Grant that I may never crave to do things impulsively, nor disdain to do what is burdensome, lest I begin things before I should or abandon them before finishing.

---

[1] *The Aquinas Prayer Book: The Prayers and Hymns of St Thomas Aquinas*, ed. Robert Anderson and Johann Moser. (Manchester: Sophia Institute Press, 2000), 33-40.

Indices

Index of Scriptural Citations
according to catechesis number

Acts 9:5	1
Deuteronomy 6:5-9	3
Genesis 29:20	3
1 Corinthians 4:1	1
John 6:44	1, 3
John 15:13	6
Luke 22:32	1
Matthew 14:27	6
Matthew 24:44	4
Matthew 5:13-14	3
Matthew 5:23-24	3
Matthew 5:48	3
Matthew 5:6	5
Matthew 7:2	5
Romans 4:18	2
2 Timothy 4:7	1

Magisterial Documents
according to catechesis number

Gaudium et spes, 34	2
Populorum Progressio, 3	3
Populorum Progressio, 23	3
Populorum Progressio, 53	3

Index of Names

according to catechesis number

Abraham	2
Alighieri, Dante	2
Aquinas, St. Thomas	2, 4, 6
Augustine of Hippo, St.	1, 2, 3
Bernard, St.	4
Borromeo, St. Charles	6
Carnegie, Andrew	2
Claver, St. Peter	3
Dupanloup, Félix	1
James, St.	2
John XXIII, St.	1, 2, 3, 4
John, St.	2
Kostka, St. Stanislaus	6
Lacordaire, Jean-Baptiste Henri-Dominique	1
Lazarus	3
Mark, St.	3
McNabb, Vincent	1
Monica of Hippo, St.	2
Nietzsche, Friedrich W.	2
Ozanam, Bl. Antoine-Frédéric	1
Paul VI, St.	1, 3
Paul, St. Vincent de	3
Pius IX, Bl.	1
Sainte-Beuve, Charles Augustin	2
Sales, St. Francis de	2, 3
Trilussa (Carlo Alberto Salustri)	1
Verne, Jules	3

Domina Nostra Publishing
555 N. Main Street, #1329
Providence, RI. 02904-5722 USA

info@DominaNostraPublishing.com

www.DominaNostraPublishing.com

www.ingramcontent.com/pod-product-compliance
Lightning Source LLC
Chambersburg PA
CBHW032051290426
44110CB00012B/1048